My Identity

By

Kirsty Holmes

CRABTREE
PUBLISHING COMPANY
WWW.CRABTREEBOOKS.COM

Published in Canada
Crabtree Publishing
616 Welland Avenue
St. Catharines, ON
L2M 5V6

Published in the United States
Crabtree Publishing
PMB 59051
350 Fifth Ave, 59th Floor
New York, NY 10118

Published by Crabtree Publishing Company in 2019

©2018 BookLife Publishing

Author: Kirsty Holmes

Editors: Holly Duhig, Janine Deschenes

Design: Jasmine Pointer

Proofreader: Melissa Boyce

**Production coordinator and
prepress technician (interior):** Margaret Amy Salter

Prepress technician (covers): Ken Wright

Print coordinator: Katherine Berti

Photographs

All images from Shutterstock

Printed in the U.S.A./122018/CG20181005

Library and Archives Canada Cataloguing in Publication

Holmes, Kirsty, author
My identity / Kirsty Holmes.

(Our values)
Includes index.
Issued in print and electronic formats.
ISBN 978-0-7787-5423-7 (hardcover).--
ISBN 978-0-7787-5446-6 (softcover).--ISBN 978-1-4271-2218-6 (HTML)

1. Identity (Psychology)--Juvenile literature. 2. Group identity--Juvenile literature. 3. Self--Juvenile literature.
I. Title.

BF697.H63 2018   j155.4'182   C2018-905485-9
                                            C2018-905486-7

Library of Congress Cataloging-in-Publication Data

Names: Holmes, Kirsty, author.
Title: My identity / Kirsty Holmes.
Description: New York : Crabtree Publishing Company, [2018] |
  Series: Our values | Includes index.
Identifiers: LCCN 2018043784 (print) | LCCN 2018045850 (ebook) |
  ISBN 9781427122186 (Electronic) |
  ISBN 9780778754237 (hardcover) |
  ISBN 9780778754466 (pbk.)
Subjects: LCSH: Identity (Psychology)--Juvenile literature. | Group
  identity--Juvenile literature. | Self--Juvenile literature.
Classification: LCC BF697 (ebook) | LCC BF697 .H544 2018 (print) |
  DDC 155.4/182--dc23
LC record available at https://lccn.loc.gov/2018043784

Contents

Words that look like **this** can be found in the glossary on page 24.

Knowing Me, Knowing You

Think of all the people you know. From their families to their interests and beliefs, they all have things that make them different from each other.

Every one of us is **unique**. Your identity is all of the things that make you who you are. It is how you see yourself.

What I Look Like

How we look is part of our identity. Do you have long hair, or short? What color eyes do you have? How tall are you?

You can show others who you are by choosing how you look. Do you like to wear clothes of your favorite color? Does your hat show the logo of your favorite sports team?

7

My Age

Grandparent

Adult

Teen

How you see yourself changes as you grow older.

Child

Baby

Your age is part of your identity. How old are you? Do you know people with different ages than you?

Your birthday is something that makes you special. It is part of your identity. On what day were you born?

My Interests

Ballet

Sports

Superheroes

We all like different things. The things we like are called our interests. Your interests make you special and unique.

Books

Brussels Sprouts

Maybe you like Brussels sprouts, reading books, or cats! What are your interests?

My Family

You are part of a family. Everyone in a family has a different **role**. Are you a brother, or maybe a sister? Are you a son, or a daughter?

Maybe, you are someone's niece or nephew. Perhaps you are **adopted**, or you live with a **foster family**. Your role in your family, and your family members, help make you who you are.

My Gender

Everyone's gender is part of their identity. Gender is how someone feels like a boy or a girl. There are many ways to feel like boys and girls.

Our looks and our likes and dislikes do not mean we are a certain gender. Everyone is unique!

My Talents

Dancers might feel that dancing is part of who they are.

Everyone is good at different things. The things we are good at are our talents. Our talents are part of our identity too.

Do you have a special talent? Maybe you are good at telling stories, solving math problems, swimming, or being kind.

My Community

Belonging to a **community** is part of your identity. You are part of the community where you live. What is your town or neighborhood called? Is it big, or small?

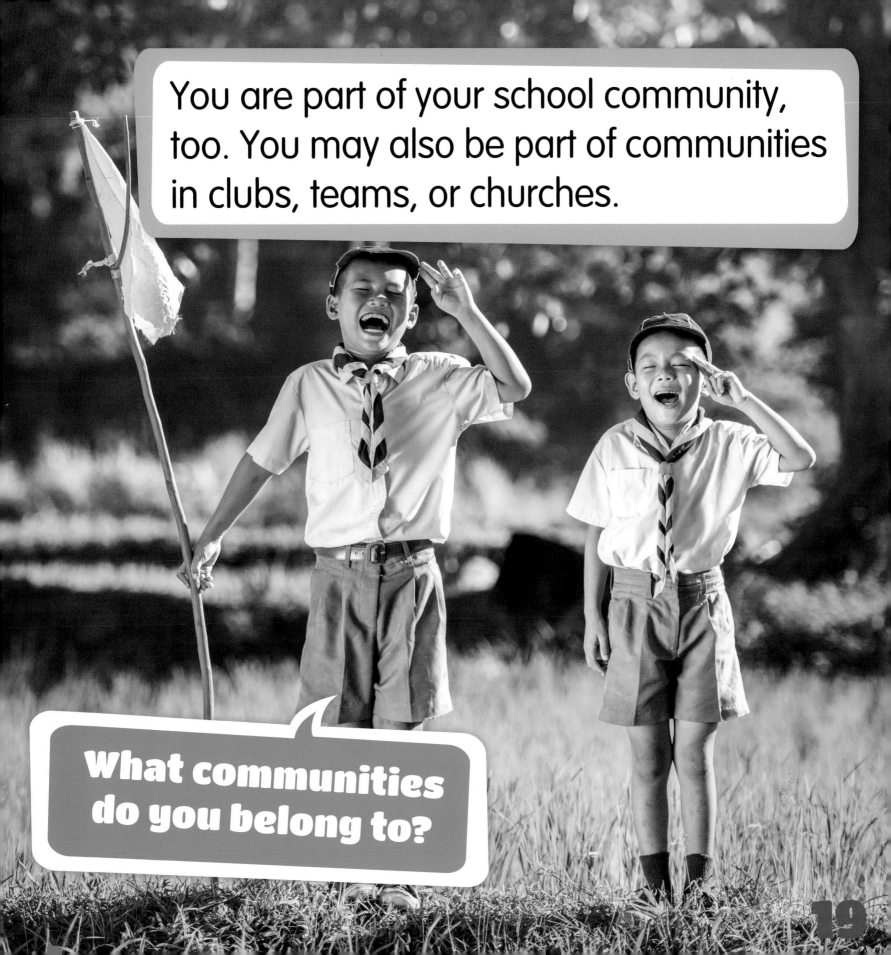

You are part of your school community, too. You may also be part of communities in clubs, teams, or churches.

What communities do you belong to?

My Beliefs

Buddhist

Hindu

Jewish

Your beliefs are part of your identity too. Beliefs often come from a religion, but they do not have to.

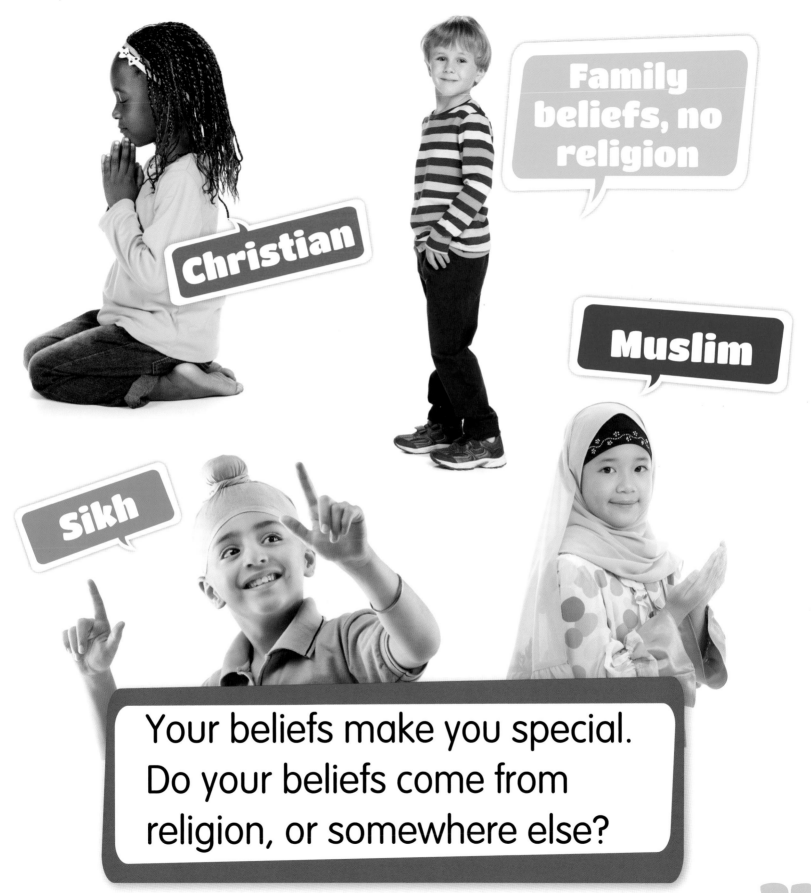

Your beliefs make you special. Do your beliefs come from religion, or somewhere else?

What is My Identity?

Think of all the things that make up your identity. Look back through this book for ideas. What makes you who you are?

Your identity makes you special and unique! Can you draw some of the things that make up your identity? Show your drawing to your friends and family.

Glossary

adopted	When a child was chosen by a family instead of born into it
community	A group of people who live, work, or play in a place
describe	Explain all about something
foster family	A family that a child lives with temporarily
logo	A symbol or picture that represents something
role	A part to play or a job to do
unique	One of a kind

Index